Mediterranean Cooking Classics

Revealed! 65 Delicious Mediterranean Diet Recipes Sure To Delight and Amaze All While Losing Inches

By Victoria Love

Top 65 Mediterranean Diet Main Dish, Lunch, One Dish, Appetizer And Salad Meals

Table of Contents

Mediterranean Tilapia Pockets

Mediterranean Chickpea Salad

Mediterranean Style Orange Roughly

Mediterranean White Bean Soup

Mediterranean Pork Chops

Mediterranean Quinoa Salad

Mediterranean Fish (Flounder)

Cod with Mediterranean Salsa

Mediterranean Pizza with Caramelized Onions

Mediterranean Fettuccine with Shrimp and Spinach

Beef & Orzo Mediterranean Style

Mediterranean Chicken Breasts with Avocado Tapenade

Mediterranean Appetizer Meals

Mediterranean Morsels

Mediterranean Bruschetta

Mediterranean Deviled Eggs

Decadent Mediterranean Honeyed Olive Oil Toasts

Mediterranean Split Pea Dip

Mediterranean Summer Breeze Shrimp Appetizer

Mediterranean Chicken Cracker Topper

Mediterranean Mayonnaise

Mediterranean Grilled Chicken Fingers

Alouette Crumbled Feta Mediterranean Caponata

Alouette Mediterranean Bruschetta

Roasted Red Pepper & Feta Dip

Mediterranean White Bean Spread with Fresh Herbs

Seven Layer Mediterranean Dip with Rosemary Butter Flatbread

Feta Cheese Log with Kalamata Olives and Sun-Dried Tomatoes

Mediterranean Salad Meals

Mediterranean Salad in Minutes

Farfalle (Bow Tie) Pasta Salad

Check Some of My Other Books

Bonus: Free Ebooks!

Mediterranean Lunch Meals

Mediterranean Scallops

Ingredients

1 tablespoon olive oil

2 teaspoons minced garlic

2 tablespoons minced shallots

1 (14 1/2 ounce) cans no-salt-added whole tomatoes (with juices)

1 (8 ounce) cans no-salt-added tomato sauce

1 tablespoon dried basil, crushed

1 pinch crushed red pepper flakes

1/4 teaspoon salt substitute

1/4 teaspoon freshly ground black pepper

1 lb sea scallops, cut crosswise in half

8 -12 ounces linguine

Directions

Take a large size frying pan, heat oil in this frying pan over moderate temperature.

Take garlic and shallots and add them to the frying pan.

Fry for one min.

Take tomatoes and chop them.

Then mix in tomatoes.

Then mix in juices.

Then mix in tomato sauce.

Then mix in herbs.

Then mix in salt.

Then mix in pepper.

Let it simmer for approximately ten min.

Then mix in scallops and keep on cooking for approximately five min or till scallops are cooked through.

Take linguine and cook it as instructed on the package.

 Then take pasta and drain it well and then divide uniformly and equally among four pasta bowls.

Use scallops mixture as topping.

Use fresh basil leaves for garnish.

Delicious.

Mediterranean Spinach Turkey Wrap

Ingredients

1/2 cup Kraft cream cheese with chives and onions

1/2 cup feta cheese, crumbled

1/4 black olives

32 inches flour tortillas

4 ounces smoked turkey, thinly sliced

1 cup loosely packed thoroughly washed spinach leaves

1/4-1/2 teaspoon oregano

Directions

Take olives and chop them up.

Take a bowl and mix in this bowl, oregano, olives, feta cheese and cream cheese, blend well.

Then take the mixture and uniformly spread it over tortilla.

Then take the turkey and place it over cream cheese mixture on half of every tortilla.

Take spinach leaves and place them over the turkey's top.

Now assemble by rolling it up.

Then use saran wrap for wrapping every sandwich.

Keep in refrigerator for a minimum of one hr.

Then unwrap it and trim every roll's ends prior to serving.

After this, take every wrap and cut into three sections.

Then diagonally cut every section into half.

Delicious.

Chocolate-Strawberry Bread Mediterranean Style

Ingredients

1 cup fresh strawberries, chopped coarsely

1 1/4 cups sugar, divided

2 eggs

1/4 cup vegetable oil

1/4 cup plain yogurt

1/4 cup pistachio nut, chopped finely

1 1/2 cups flour

1/2 teaspoon baking soda

1/4 teaspoon salt

1 teaspoon cinnamon

1/2 teaspoon vanilla

1/2 cup dates, chopped

1 ounce bittersweet chocolate, melted

Directions

Take strawberries and add 1/8 C of sugar to the strawberries. Allow to stand.

Then take rest of sugar and beat with yogurt along with oil and eggs.

Then mix in pistachio nuts.

Take flour, soda and sift them together with cinnamon, salt. After this blend into the mixture of sugar.

Then mix in vanilla.

Then mix in dates.

Then mix in strawberries along with juice.

Then finally, mix in melted chocolate.

Then take the mixture and pour it into loaf pan that has been sprayed with nonstick spray.

Then bake for approximately FIFTY to sixty min, at 350 degrees Fahrenheit.

Mediterranean Roast Peppers

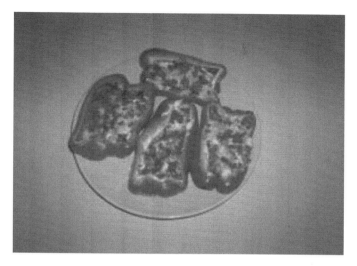

Ingredients

4 small red peppers, halved, cored and seeded

3 tablespoons capers, chopped

10 -12 black olives, pitted and chopped

2 garlic cloves, finely chopped

2 -3 ounces mozzarella cheese, grated

1 -1 1/2 ounce fresh white breadcrumbs

1/2 cup dry white wine

3 tablespoons olive oil

1 teaspoon finely chopped fresh mint

1 teaspoon chopped fresh parsley

Fresh ground black pepper

Directions

First, heat the oven to three hundred fifty (350) degrees Fahrenheit.

Then ovenproof dish and butter it's shallow.

Then take the peppers and place them tightly in the dish.

Use chopped capers, black olives, garlic, mozzarella, breadcrumbs as sprinkles.

Then take it and pour it over wine as well as olive oil.

Use mint, parsley, ground black pepper as sprinkles.

Then bake for thirty to forty min till crunchy and golden brown in color.

Mediterranean Cheese Fold overs

Ingredients

Fold overs

1 (6 ounce) containers crumbled feta cheese with garlic and herbs (1 1/4 cups)

2 ounces finely shredded Romano cheese

1/4 cup finely chopped green onion (4 medium)

2 tablespoons finely chopped ripe olives

1 egg

1 egg, separated

1 (16 1/3 ounce) cans refrigerated buttermilk biscuits

1 teaspoon water

2 teaspoons sesame seeds

Garnish

1 sprig fresh parsley

1 whole ripe olives

Directions

Heat the oven to three hundred fifty(350) degrees Fahrenheit.

Then take cookie sheet and lightly grease it with shortening.

Take a medium size bowl, and blend olives, onions, and both cheeses in this bowl. Mash well.

Then mix in one egg.

Then mix in one egg white.

Blend till well mixed.

Take dough and separate it into eight biscuits. After this, separate every biscuit into two layers and form sixteen biscuit rounds. Then press each three inch round shape.

Take one tablespoon of cheese mixture and spoon onto every dough round's center.

Right after this, fold dough in half over filling; seal the edges.

After this, put on the cookie sheet that has been greased.

Then take a small size bowl, beat water, egg yolk in this bowl till well mixed.

Then after this, brush over dough fold overs.

Use sesame seed as sprinkle over each one.

Finally, bake for sixteen to twenty min at 350 degrees Fahrenheit till color changes to golden brown. Then move to plate after removing from cookie sheet.

Use parsley as garnish along with couple of olives.

Mediterranean Veggie Wrap

Ingredients

1 soft cracker bread, halved (Lavosh) or 1 large flour tortilla

4 ounces hummus

1/4 cup fresh parsley, chopped

8 ripe olives, sliced

1 small cucumber, thinly sliced

1 small tomato, seeded and chopped

1 ounce feta cheese, crumbled

Directions

First, take hummus and spread on bread.

Take parsley, cucumber and add them.

Then take olives, tomatoes and add them.

Then take cheese and add it.

Finally, roll it up and eat it.

Mediterranean Chicken Salad Sandwiches

Ingredients

4 boneless chicken breast halves

1/2 cup water

1 teaspoon dried basil leaves

1/4 teaspoon salt

1/4 teaspoon pepper

1 cup cucumber, chopped

1/2 cup mayonnaise

1/4 cup chopped roasted red pepper

1/4 cup sliced pitted black olives

1/4 cup yogurt

1/4 teaspoon garlic powder

6 Kaiser Rolls, split

Additional mayonnaise

Lettuce leaf

Directions

Take a medium size pan and put chicken along with water, basil, salt and pepper in this pan. Heat to boiling.

Then lower the temperature and let it simmer for ten to twelve min, covered, or till pink color disappears from the centre of the chicken.

Then let it cool by removing the chicken from pan.

Then chop into half inch pieces.

Take a medium size bowl, and combine garlic powder, yogurt, olives, chicken, cucumber, mayonnaise, olives and red pepper in this bowl. Toss well.

Then take rolls and spread them with extra mayonnaise.

Use lettuce and chicken salad mixture as toppings.

Mediterranean Tuna Sandwiches

Ingredients

4 teaspoons roasted red pepper olive oil

4 teaspoons balsamic vinegar

8 slices whole grain bread or 8 slices pita bread

2 (6 ounce) cans tuna in water, drained and flaked

1/3 cup sun-dried tomato packed in oil, drained

1/4 cup ripe green olives or 1/4 cup ripe olives, sliced

1/4 cup red onions or 1/4 cup sweet Spanish onion, finely chopped

1/4 cup red bell pepper, finely chopped (optional)

3 tablespoons mayonnaise (optional) or 3 tablespoons low-fat mayonnaise (optional)

2 teaspoons capers (more to taste)

1/4 teaspoon fresh ground black pepper

4 romaine lettuce leaves or 4 curly green lettuce leaves

Directions

Take a small size bowl and combine in this bowl, vinegar, and olive oil.

Then take the oil mixture and brush it uniformly over one side of every bread slice or you can brush the oil mixture inside the pita pockets.

Take tuna along with rest of ingredients and combine them together, besides lettuce.

Then take one lettuce leaf and place it on every four bread slices.

Then lettuce and top it with tuna mixture. Then cover with the rest of bread slices.

Mediterranean Salad

Ingredients

1/3 cup olive oil

2 tablespoons balsamic vinegar

1 teaspoon Dijon mustard

1 garlic clove, minced

1 pinch salt

1 pinch pepper

2 (19 ounce) cans chickpeas, rinsed (or white kidney beans)

1/2 red pepper, julienned

1 green pepper, julienned

1/2 cup stuffed green olive

2 tablespoons capers (optional)

Directions

Take olive oil, salt, pepper, garlic, mustard, vinegar and WHISK THESE ingredients together.

Take the rest of ingredients and add them.

Then fold together.

You can serve this recipe over greens.

Mediterranean Kalamata Hummus

Ingredients

1 1/2 cups garbanzo beans, rinsed and drained

1/4 cup tahini

2 garlic cloves

1/4 cup fresh lemon juice

1 teaspoon cayenne (reserve a 1/4 tsp. For topping)

4 tablespoons olive oil (reserve 2 tablespoons for topping)

3/4 cup Kalamata olive

2 tablespoons capers

1 small red bell pepper, seeded and sliced

1 teaspoon ground cumin (reserve 1/4 teaspoon for topping)

3 tablespoons fresh parsley (reserve 1 tablespoon for topping)

Directions

Take all of the ingredients and puree them in either a blender or food processor.

Take cold water and add enough of it.

Then take puree and spoon onto shallow plate.

Then USE the rest of olive oil and stew with the rest of parsley as drizzle.

Use rest of cumin and cayenne as sprinkles.

Enjoy!

Mediterranean One Dish Meals

Mediterranean Tilapia Pockets

Ingredients

4 tilapia fillets

4 tablespoons extra virgin olive oil, divided

1 tablespoon all purpose Greek seasoning, divided

4 slices prosciutto

1/3 cup grape tomatoes, chopped

1/3 cup zucchini, chopped

10 -12 olives, sliced

1 tablespoon capers

1 tablespoon Italian parsley, chopped

1 tablespoon mint, chopped

1 tablespoon lemon juice

1 teaspoon lemon zest

4 teaspoons goat cheese

1 teaspoon black pepper

4 sheets Reynolds Wrap Foil, sheets 12x10. 75

Directions

First, heat the oven to 375 degrees Fahrenheit.

Take filets and rub them with half of the olive oil and half of the Greek seasoning.

Then take one slice of prosciutto and wrap it around every filet.

Then take one filet and place it on one aluminum foil sheet.

Take a small size mixing bowl and combine in it, olives, rest of spice, zest, lemon juice, min, parsley, capers, zucchini and tomatoes.

Toss well.

Take same quantity of tomato mixture and place it over the top of every filet.

Use goat cheese as well as black pepper for topping.

Then seal the filet.

Then take aluminum pockets and place them on large size oven proof sheet pan.

Finally, bake for fifteen to twenty min, then unseal it after resting for five min.

Mediterranean Fish (Flounder)

Ingredients

5 roma tomatoes, chopped or 1 (15 ounce) cans chopped tomatoes

2 tablespoons olive oil

1/2 onion, chopped

2 garlic cloves, chopped

1 pinch Italian seasoning

1/4 cup white wine

24 Kalamata olives, pitted and chopped

4 tablespoons capers

1 teaspoon lemon juice, fresh preferred

6 leaves fresh basil, chopped

3 tablespoons parmesan cheese

1 lb flounder or 1 lb sole or 1 lb halibut or 1 lb. Mahi Mahi or 1 lb tilapia fillet

Directions

First, heat the oven to 425 degrees Fahrenheit.

Then after this, prepare tomatoes if in case fresh by placing them into boiling water, then take them out and move them to a bowl of ice water and don't forget to peel the skins.

Take olive oil and heat it in medium size frying over moderate temperature.

Take onions and add them. Fry till soften.

Take garlic, Italian seasoning and add them, mix well.

Add tomatoes and cook till soften.

Then blend in wine.

Then blend in capers.

Then blend in olives.

Then blend in lemon juice.

Then blend in half of the basil.

Lower the temperature.

Then stir in parmesan cheese.

Then cook till mixture is bubbly.

Take fish and place it in a shallow baking dish.

Use sauce mixture for covering the fish.

Then bake for fifteen to twenty min.

Your delicious recipe is ready.

Mediterranean Fettuccine with Shrimp and Spinach

Ingredients

1 cup sour cream

1/2 cup crumbled feta cheese

1/4 teaspoon crushed red pepper flakes

1 teaspoon salt

3 garlic cloves, peeled and chopped

2 teaspoons dried basil, crushed

8 ounces fettuccine pasta, uncooked

1 (10 ounce) packages frozen spinach, thawed

12 ounces medium shrimp (uncooked, peeled, & deveined)

Directions

Take basil, garlic, salt, red pepper, feta, sour cream and combine them together.

Keep aside.

Then prepare fettuccine as instructed on the package but after this, eight min of cooking, take spinach, shrimp and add them to boiling water/pasta.

Then boil for two extra min.

Drain well completely.

Take pasta/shrimp mixture and add them to sour cream mixture, toss well.

Serve right away.

Mediterranean Scallops

Ingredients

1 tablespoon olive oil

2 teaspoons minced garlic

2 tablespoons minced shallots

1 (14 1/2 ounce) cans no-salt-added whole tomatoes (with juices)

1 (8 ounce) cans no-salt-added tomato sauce

1 tablespoon dried basil, crushed

1 pinch crushed red pepper flakes

1/4 teaspoon salt substitute

1/4 teaspoon freshly ground black pepper

1 lb sea scallops, cut crosswise in half

8 -12 ounces linguine

Directions

First, heat oil in large size frying pan over moderate temperature.

Take shallots, garlic and add them. Fry for one min.

Take tomatoes and chop them.

Then mix in tomatoes and juice.

Then mix in tomato sauce.

Then mix in herbs.

Then mix in salt.

Then mix in pepper.

Then allow to simmer for approximately ten min.

Then blend in scallops.

Keep on cooking for approximately five min or till scallops are cooked through.

Then take linguine and cook it as instructed on the package.

Then drain pasta well. And divide equally among three to four pasta bowls.

Use scallops mixture as topping.

Use fresh basil leaves for garnish.

You can serve this delicious recipe with tossed green salad and Italian bread.

Mediterranean Tuna Sandwich

Ingredients

1/4 cup olive oil

1/2 cup red wine vinegar

1 red onion, sliced very thinly

1 can tuna

Capers

Sliced Kalamata olive, to taste

1 fresh tomato, sliced 1/4-inch thick (or several cherry tomatoes)

Leafy greens (romaine hearts or spinach work well)

Fresh bread

Directions

Take olive oil, red wine vinegar and blend them together in small size bowl.

Take onions and place them in mixture and allow to marinate while preparing the remaining components/ingredients.

Once ready, then set out bottom bread slice, use oil-vinegar mixture for thinly drizzle the slice.

Make a layer of onions.

Then layer capers and olives.

Then layer tuna.

Then layer tomato.

Then layer leaf green.

Use oil-vinegar mixture for thinly drizzle

Use another bread slice for topping.

Then right after this, squish everything together and allow to rest for a couple of min.

Delicious.

Mediterranean Veggie Lasagna

Ingredients

1 1/2 tablespoons olive oil

1 (10 ounce) packages frozen artichoke hearts, thawed and sliced

2 (14 ounce) cans black olives, halved

1 red onion, chopped

3 stalks celery, diced

10 green onions, sliced

2 small zucchini, diced

1 large roasted red pepper, diced

1 (10 ounce) packages frozen spinach, thawed

2 tablespoons fresh diced garlic

2 lbs asparagus, trimmed and chopped into 1/2 inch pieces

10 ounces sun-dried tomatoes packed in oil, drained and diced

3 tablespoons fresh sweet basil, chopped

15 lasagna noodles, cooked according to package instructions

8 ounces asiago cheese, shredded (or feta if you would prefer)

6 tablespoons butter

1/2 cup flour

5 cups milk

Directions

First, heat the oven to 375.

Take oil and heat it in large size pot over moderately high temperature.

Take red onion and add it.

Then take green onion and add it.

Then take garlic and add it.

Then take celery and add it.

Quick fry till onion is translucent and celery is about to tender.

Take other vegetables and add them one after another. Don't to mix prior to add the next vegetable.

Then cook for five min, covered, mix one time.

Then cook till veggies are soften for approximately ten min extra, uncovered, stir frequently.

Use salt and pepper for seasonings.

Take butter and melt it in large size saucepan over moderate temperature.

Then take flour and whisk it in for two min.

Then take milk and whisk it in.

Then cook till mixture boils, whisk frequently.

Take away from heat and use salt, pepper as seasonings.

Then take one cup of sauce and spoon it over lasagna pan's bottom.

Take five lasagna noodles and arrange them on the top of sauce.

Take half of the veggies and spoon it over noodles.

Take 1.5 cups of sauce and spoon it over vegetables.

Use one-third cheese as sprinkle over sauce.

Replicate every layer one time.

Use the final five lasagna noodles as topping.

Take the rest of sauce and spoon it over noodles.

Use the rest of cheese as topping.

You can keep it in refrigerator for later use, cover it tightly and firmly.

Bake it uncovered on the middle rack till sauce is bubbling.

Take out from oven and let it rest for a minimum of ten min prior to slicing.

Chicken Bake Mediterranean Style

Ingredients

1 tablespoon olive oil

600 g chicken drumsticks (6 small)

1 1/4 kg chicken thighs, cutlets (6)

1 kg small potato, halved

2 ripe tomatoes, finely chopped

95 g Kalamata olives

2 garlic cloves, peeled, thinly sliced

2 sprigs fresh rosemary, leaves picked

125 ml dry white wine

Flaked sea salt

Fresh ground black pepper

Directions

Heat the oven to two hundred (200) degrees Fahrenheit.

Take oil and heat it in ovenproof baking dish over moderate temperature.

Take chicken drumsticks and add them, and cook for five min, mix frequently or till color is brown all over.

Then shift to plate.

Use foil for foiling and to keep warm.

You can replicate with chicken thigh cutlets.

Take potatoes and add to dish, then cook for five min, turn frequently or till golden in color.

Take away from heat.

Take chicken and add to the potato in the dish.

Use tomato, olives, garlic as toppings.

Use rosemary as sprinkle.

Then pour over the wine.

Use salt, pepper as seasonings.

Bake for forty five min, or till chicken is cooked through.

Delicious.

Rigatoni Mediterranean

Ingredients

1 lb. rigatoni pasta (uncooked)

1/4 cup olive oil, divided

5 1/2 cups eggplants, diced and peeled (about 1 large)

1 large zucchini

2 cups sweet onions, thinly sliced (about 1 large onion)

3/4 cup scallion, thinly sliced

1/4 cup fresh basil, chopped

1 teaspoon Italian seasoning

1/2 teaspoon salt

1/2 teaspoon black pepper

1 (28 ounce) cans crushed tomatoes, undrained

8 ounces part-skim mozzarella cheese, shredded

1/2 cup parmesan cheese, fresh and grated

Directions

First, heat the oven to three hundred fifty (350) degrees Fahrenheit.

Prepare pasta as instructed on the package.

Drain well and keep aside.

Take two tablespoons of oil and heat it in large size nonstick frying over moderately high temperature.

Take eggplant and add to pan.

Fry for approximately six min or till color is light brown.

Then drain well on paper towel.

Take the rest of two tablespoons of oil and heat it in pan over moderate temperature.

Take garlic and add to pan and cook for thirty seconds, mix continuously.

Take onion, zucchini, and scallions and add them to pan.

Then cook for approximately six min or till soften, mix frequently.

Take chopped basil, salt, pepper, tomatoes, Italian seasoning and add them.

Heat to boiling.

Lower the temperature and let it simmer for approximately fifteen min, covered.

Take tomato mixture, eggplant, pasta and combine them in large size bowl.

Then blend in shredded mozzarella.

Then move to baking dish that has been coated with cooking spray.

Use parmesan as sprinkle.

Then bake for fifteen min at 350 degrees Fahrenheit, covered.

Then uncover it and bake for extra five min

Delicious recipe is ready

French Roast Chicken and Mediterranean Vegetables in Wine

Ingredients

1 organic roasting chickens or 4 lbs chicken pieces or 6 chicken breasts, skin on and bone in

1 tablespoon olive oil

4 fluid ounces dry white wine

Salt and black pepper

Fresh thyme or fresh rosemary

Roasted vegetables

Directions

First things first, prepare a batch of French Roast Vegetables with Hot Balsamic and Olive Oil Dressing.

Then after this, heat the oven to 360 degrees.

Take a sturdy tin and grease it with a little bit of olive oil.

Take the remaining olive oil and brush it over the chicken pieces.

Use salt, black pepper as seasonings.

Take fresh thyme and place it over the chicken's top. Then roast in for approximately forty five min to sixty min, it depends on the chicken pieces.

Then take out from oven and drain well.

Take the roasted veggies and wine and add them to chicken.

Then blend through and turn up the oven to four hundred fifty (450) degrees Fahrenheit.

Take the chicken, veggies and put them back in the oven for roasting for fifteen to twenty five min extra min till chicken becomes crunchy, golden brown in color and the meat falls off.

Delicious recipe is ready.

Mediterranean Pork with Orzo

Ingredients

1 1/2 lbs pork tenderloin

1 teaspoon lemon pepper

2 tablespoons olive oil

3 quarts water

1 1/4 cups orzo pasta

1/4 teaspoon salt

6 ounces fresh spinach

1 cup grape tomatoes, halved

1/2 cup Kalamata olive, chopped

3/4 cup feta cheese

Directions

First, take water, salt and heat them to boiling.

Take orzo and add it, then cook for eight min.

Take pork and chop it into one inch cubes. Toss well with lemon pepper.

Take olive oil and heat it in frying pan, fry the pork for approximately eight to ten min, or till ready and done.

Lower the temperature.

Then take tomatoes, spinach, olives and add them.

Then cook for two min or till spinach is wilted.

Right after this, drain orzo well, don't forget to toss with pork mixture.

Finally, use feta for topping.

Mediterranean Main Dish Meals

Mediterranean Scampi

Ingredients

2 lbs large shrimp, peeled, deveined, tails on

1/4 lb unsalted butter

1 head garlic, whole head, peeled, crushed, and chopped fine

1 cup green onion, bulbs and stems chopped coarse

2 large red bell peppers, roasted, skin seeds and pith removed and cut into thin strips

2 cups fresh ripe plum tomatoes, peeled and cut up with their juice

1 cup flat-leaf Italian parsley, with stems (chopped fine)

1 tablespoon fresh oregano leaves, chopped fine

1 tablespoon fresh basil leaf, chopped fine

1/2 cup Kalamata olive, pitted, crushed and chopped coarse

1/4 cup capers

2 -3 lemons, cut into wedges

1/2 lemon, juice of

1/2 cup dry white wine

Directions

First, take a large size frying pan, melt butter in this pan.

Quick fry garlic, till color changes to golden and then take out from the frying and keep aside.

Take onions and add them, then fry till soften, then take away from heat and keep aside.

Take plum tomatoes and add them along with their juice.

Then take white wine, lemon juice and add them.

Heat to boiling.

Then take onion and garlic (which you got in previous steps) and add them.

Take roasted red bell peppers and add them.

Lower the temperature and let the liquid to reduce.

Take parsley, basil, oregano and add them.

Then after this, add shrimp and steak till pink in color.

Take caper, olives and add them.

Once ready, shift them to serving bowl, use lemon wedges as garnish.

Mediterranean Chicken Breasts

Ingredients

1/2 cup pecorino Romano cheese, grated

1/4 cup dry breadcrumbs

1 teaspoon dried basil

1/4 teaspoon dried garlic

1/4 teaspoon paprika

1/4 teaspoon sea salt or 1/4 teaspoon salt, to taste

1/4 teaspoon fresh ground black pepper or 1/4 teaspoon fresh ground black pepper, to taste

3 tablespoons olive oil

6 large boneless skinless chicken breast halves

Directions

First, take the 1st seven ingredients and blend them together on waxed paper piece.

Then take the chicken breast halves and dip them in oil, after this, coat them with breadcrumb mixture.

Take a nonstick frying pan and spray it with cooking spray, then add chicken to the frying pan and cook for fifteen min, turn one time, or till color changes to golden brown.

Roasted Mediterranean Vegetables

Ingredients

12 ounces potatoes, cut into 1 1/2-inch chunks

1 small eggplant, sliced and quartered

2 bell peppers, chopped into 1-inch squares

1 cup red onion, sliced

2 tablespoons olive oil

2 tablespoons balsamic vinegar

1/2 teaspoon basil

1/2 teaspoon oregano

1/2 teaspoon chives

4 garlic cloves, minced

Salt and pepper, to taste

Directions

First, heat the oven to 425 degrees Fahrenheit.

Take shallow roasting dish and prepare is with nonstick cooking spray.

Then take potatoes, red onion slices and combine them with eggplant, both bell peppers, then put them in roasting dish.

Then take olive oil, basil, oregano and whisk them with balsamic vinegar, chives, salt, pepper and garlic.

Then take sauce and drizzle over mixed veggies and toss well.

Then roast the veggies for approximately forty five min, or till soften.

Mix once half cooking time is passed.

Mediterranean Tilapia Pockets

Ingredients

4 tilapia fillets

4 tablespoons extra virgin olive oil, divided

1 tablespoon all purpose Greek seasoning, divided

4 slices prosciutto

1/3 cup grape tomatoes, chopped

1/3 cup zucchini, chopped

10 -12 olives, sliced

1 tablespoon capers

1 tablespoon Italian parsley, chopped

1 tablespoon mint, chopped

1 tablespoon lemon juice

1 teaspoon lemon zest

4 teaspoons goat cheese

1 teaspoon black pepper

4 sheets Reynolds Wrap Foil, sheets 12x10. 75

Directions

First, heat the oven to 375 degrees Fahrenheit.

Take filets and rub with half of the olive oil and half of the Greek seasoning.

Take one slice of prosciutto and wrap it around each filet.

Then take that filet and put on one sheet of aluminum foil.

Take a small size mixing bowl, and combine in this bowl, parsley, mint, lemon juice, tomatoes, zucchini, olives, capers, & zest and rest of spice blend.

Toss well.

Take equal quantity of tomato mixture and put it on top of every filet.

Use goat cheese and black pepper for topping.

Then seal the filet with foil.

Then take these aluminum pockets and place them on large size oven proof sheet pan.

Then bake for fifteen to twenty min. let rest for five min.

Finally, unseal and serve deliciously.

Mediterranean Chickpea Salad

Ingredients

15 ounces chickpeas, rinsed and drained

1 cucumber, finely chopped

1 cup grape tomatoes, halved

1/4 cup sweet onion, finely chopped

1 garlic clove, minced

1 1/2 tablespoons fresh parsley, minced

2 tablespoons fresh basil, chopped

4 ounces mozzarella cheese, cubed

1 tablespoon olive oil

2 tablespoons balsamic vinegar

1/4 teaspoon sea salt

4 cups mixed salad greens (optional)

Directions

First, take medium size bowl, and combine in this bowl, chickpeas, cucumber, tomatoes, onion, garlic, parsley, and basil and mozzarella cheese.

Take olive oil, vinegar, salt and drizzle over the top. Toss well all of the ingredients.

Then cover the bowl and keep in refrigerator for sixty min.

Delicious.

Mediterranean Style Orange Roughly

Ingredients

4 (6 ounce) orange roughy fillets, 1/2 inch thick

4 ounces feta cheese with dried basil and tomato or 4 ounces plain feta cheese

1/4 cup low-fat sour cream

1/4 cup finely chopped red onion

1 garlic clove, minced finely

3 tablespoons capers, drained and rinsed

2 small plum tomatoes, seeded, and finely chopped

2 teaspoon lemons, rind of, grated

1 teaspoon dried oregano

1/2 teaspoon fresh ground black pepper

1/2 teaspoon kosher salt

1 -2 teaspoon white wine (optional)

Directions

First, heat the oven to four hundred (400) Degrees Fahrenheit.

Use foil for lining the baking sheet.

Use nonstick spray for spraying the foil.

Use kosher salt, fresh ground pepper for seasoning the both sides of the fish.

Take a medium size bowl, and combine in this bowl, garlic, capers, tomatoes, lemon peel and oregano, feta, sour cream, red onion and mix till completely blended.

Take wine and add it to feta cheese mixture if you like.

Take fish and arrange on the already prepared baking sheet.

Take cheese topping and spread it over fish.

Then bake for ten to twelve min or till cooked through.

Mediterranean White Bean Soup

Ingredients

4 cups vegetable broth

1 medium potato, peeled and diced small

1 large carrot, peeled and diced small

1 tablespoon olive oil

1 medium onion, chopped

3 cloves garlic, minced

4 cups cooked cannellini beans or 2 (14 ounce) cans canned cannellini, drained and rinsed

1/2 teaspoon dried thyme

1/4 teaspoon dried rosemary

Salt & freshly ground black pepper

1 teaspoon lemon juice

Directions

First, take two cups of broth and heat them to boiling in large size saucepan.

Take potatoes, carrots and add them, cover, and lower the temperature and allow to simmer gently for fifteen min.

Then take oil and place it in heavy soup pot over moderately high temperature.

Take onions and add them, lower the temperature to LOW, cover it and cook for ten min, mix frequently.

Take garlic and add it and cook for sixty seconds.

Then take one cup of broth and add it and heat to boiling.

Take cooked/prepared potatoes, carrots along with their liquid and ADD THEM.

Then mix in thyme.

Then mix in rosemary.

Take a food processor and puree the beans in the processor along with final cup of broth.

Then add to the soup and heat to boiling.

Use salt, pepper as seasonings.

Then mix in lemon juice.

You can serve this recipe croutons or toasted bread as garnish.

Mediterranean Pork Chops

Ingredients

Pork Chops

1 lb thin boneless pork loin chop

Cooking spray, to coat

Garlic salt, to taste

Ground black pepper, to taste

Sauce

1 teaspoon olive oil

1 cup red onion, chopped

2 garlic cloves, minced

1 lemon, juice of

1 tablespoon balsamic vinegar

1 tablespoon whole grain Dijon mustard

1/4 teaspoon sea salt

1/4 teaspoon ground black pepper

1/2 teaspoon dried oregano

2 (1 ounce) packets Splenda sugar substitute (if too acidic) or 2 (1 ounce) packets sugar, to taste (if too acidic)

2 tablespoons capers

8 ounces grape tomatoes, whole

1/2 cup pitted Kalamata olive, whole

Toppings

2 tablespoons fresh parsley, chopped to top

Feta cheese, to top (optional)

Directions

Take pork chops and coat them with spray oil.

Use garlic salt and pepper as sprinkles on both sides of pork chops.

Then cook and put in plate.

Meanwhile you are preparing pork chops, prepare the sauce.

Take olive oil and heat it in small size frying pan over moderate temperature.

Then take red onion and add, fry for five min.

Take garlic and add it, fry for two additional min.

Take the remaining ingredients and add them to olives. Fry for next three to five min or till heated through.

Take sauce and pour it over prepared pork chops.

If you like, use parsley and feta as toppings.

Mediterranean Quinoa Salad

Ingredients

1 cup quinoa or 1 cup bulgur

2 cups water

Marinade

4 tablespoons orange juice, freshly squeezed

3 tablespoons lemon juice, freshly squeezed

2 tablespoons olive oil

1 -2 tablespoon balsamic vinegar or 1 -2 tablespoon wine vinegar

1 teaspoon brown sugar or 1 teaspoon raw sugar

1/2 teaspoon garlic powder (or to taste)

Salt, to taste

Fresh ground black pepper, to taste

1/2 cup finely chopped fresh basil leaf

Vegetables

1/3 cup finely chopped sun-dried tomato

2 red onions, finely chopped or 8 -10 green onions, chopped

1 lb cherry tomatoes, cut in half

6 ounces black olives, sliced

3/4 cup pine nuts (toasted)

Directions

Take quinoa and rinse it in strainer under running water.

Drain well.

Heat to boiling.

Then take quinoa and add it and allow to simmer for ten to fifteen min.

Keep aside to cool.

Take the marinade ingredients and combine them well. Then pour over quinoa that has been cooled. Mix well.

Take veggies, herbs and add them. Mix once again.

Use pine nuts as sprinkle.

Then cover it and keep in refrigerator for two to six hours

Mediterranean Fish (Flounder)

Ingredients

5 roma tomatoes, chopped or 1 (15 ounce) cans chopped tomatoes

2 tablespoons olive oil

1/2 onion, chopped

2 garlic cloves, chopped

1 pinch Italian seasoning

1/4 cup white wine

24 Kalamata olives, pitted and chopped

4 tablespoons capers

1 teaspoon lemon juice, fresh preferred

6 leaves fresh basil, chopped

3 tablespoons parmesan cheese

1 lb flounder or 1 lb sole or 1 lb halibut or 1 lb. Mahi Mahi or 1 lb tilapia fillet

Directions

First, heat the oven to 425 degrees Fahrenheit.

Take tomatoes and chop them with skins.

Take medium size frying pan and heat olive oil in it over moderate temperature.

Take onions and add them, fry till soften.

Take garlic, Italian seasoning and add them. Mix well.

Take tomatoes and add them. Cook till soften.

Then blend in wine.

Then blend in olives.

Then blend in capers.

Then blend in lemon juice.

Then blend in half of the basil.

Lower the temperature, mix in parmesan cheese.

Then cook for approximately fifteen min or till mixture is bubbly.

Take fish and place it in shallow baking dish.

Use sauce mixture for covering and bake for fifteen to twenty min, once done, the fish should flake easily with fork.

Cod with Mediterranean Salsa

Ingredients

Salsa

1/3 cup Kalamata olive, pitted and diced

1 plum tomato, peeled, seeded, and diced

1 shallot, minced

1 tablespoon fresh basil, minced

1 tablespoon capers

1/4 teaspoon grated orange zest

1 teaspoon fresh lemon juice

1 teaspoon olive oil

Salt

Pepper

Cod

1 lb cod fish fillet

Lemon pepper

Salt

Cooking spray

1 teaspoon olive oil

Directions

Take all of the salsa components/ingredients and blend them together.

Then take fish and pat it dry.

Use salt, lemon pepper as seasoning.

Take a nonstick frying pan and spray it with cooking spray, then heat over moderately high temperature.

Take olive oil and add it to pan, and heat it.

Then cook filets four min on every side till ready and done.

You can serve this recipe with salsa spooned over top.

Mediterranean Pizza with Caramelized Onions

Ingredients

Caramelized Onions

1/4 cup olive oil

3 lbs sweet onions, sliced thin

8 garlic cloves, pressed

2 tablespoons fresh thyme or 2 teaspoons dried thyme, crushed

1 tablespoon fresh oregano or 1 teaspoon dried oregano, crushed

2 bay leaves

Salt

Pepper

Eggplant

8 ounces eggplants, peeled, diced into 1/2 inch cubes

2 medium roma tomatoes, peeled and diced

1 tablespoon fresh basil or 1 teaspoon dried basil, crushed

1 tablespoon olive oil

1 tablespoon capers, drained and rinsed

Pepper

Crust

1 cup warm water

1 tablespoon yeast

1/8 teaspoon sugar

2 tablespoons olive oil

1/2 teaspoon salt

1 1/2 cups whole wheat pastry flour

1 1/2 cups all-purpose flour

Toppings

4 tablespoons olive oil, divided

1 teaspoon fresh marjoram or 1/4 teaspoon dried marjoram

1 teaspoon fresh basil or 1/4 teaspoon dried basil

1 teaspoon fresh oregano or 1/4 teaspoon dried oregano

1 cup feta cheese, crumbled

2 red bell peppers, roasted, peeled and cut into thin strips

1/3 cup Kalamata olive, pitted, sliced in half lengthwise

1/2 cup Parmigiano-Reggiano cheese, grated

Red pepper flakes

Directions

Take a heavy frying pan and heat olive oil in the pan.

Then take onions, garlic, herbs and add them, caramelize onions.

Then cook over low temperature for forty five min or till onion is tender. Get rid of the bay leaf.

Then take salt, pepper and add them according to your taste and choice.

Now for roasting bell peppers, core and chop in half and then put on broiler pan while the skin side up. Put the peppers under already heated broiler for ten to fifteen min. then take the cooked peppers and place them in a paper bag, fold top closed. And let it cool for ten min. once cool, remove the skin and slice them into fine strips.

Now for roasting eggplant and tomatoes, heat the oven to four HUNDRED (400) degrees Fahrenheit.

Use nonstick cooking spray for spraying the ovenproof pan.

Take capers, basil, tomatoes, eggplant and add them. Then use olive oil for drizzling. The put in the oven and cook for thirty min, mix one or two time. Once prepared and cooked, add pepper according to your taste and choice.

Now for topping, take fresh herbs and finely mince them, then take these herbs and add them to three tablespoons of olive oil. Keep aside while you are preparing crust.

Take a small size bowl, use yeast, sugar as sprinkles over one cup of warm water. Mix well.

Let it stand for five min.

Then take a medium size bowl, combine in this bowl, the flours and measure 1 1/2 cups; keep aside.

Take salt and add to the rest of one and half cups of flour.

Then mix in yeast.

Then mix in oil.

Take the reserved flour and add it till dough is soften.

Knead till smooth enough.

Then place in bowl and before that, lightly oil it with olive oil.

Let it rise for TWENTLY min.

Heat the oven to 475 degrees Fahrenheit. Take large size pizza pan and oil it with olive oil.

Then take dough and turn it onto lightly floured surface and knead for eight to ten min, after this, roll into your preferred size. Form the crust around the corners and edges by stretching the dough to the sides of pan.

Then brush the dough with herb mixture as well as olive oil.

Use crumbled feta cheese as topping, along with onions, eggplant mixture, bell peppers and olives.

Use parmesan cheese as sprinkle all over.

Then use one tablespoon olive oil for drizzle.

Then bake for fifteen to twenty min or till the color of crust becomes light brown.

Delicious.

Mediterranean Fettuccine with Shrimp and Spinach

Ingredients

1 cup sour cream

1/2 cup crumbled feta cheese

1/4 teaspoon crushed red pepper flakes

1 teaspoon salt

3 garlic cloves, peeled and chopped

2 teaspoons dried basil, crushed

8 ounces fettuccine pasta, uncooked

1 (10 ounce) packages frozen spinach, thawed

12 ounces medium shrimp (uncooked, peeled, & deveined)

Directions

First, take basil, garlic, salt, red pepper, feta, sour cream and combine them together. And keep aside.

Then cook fettuccine as instructed on package.

After eight min, add spinach as well as shrimp to boiling water/pasta. Then boil for approximately two extra min.

Drain well and completely.

Then take hot pasta/shrimp mixture and add to sour cream mixture, toss gently.

Serve right away.

Beef & Orzo Mediterranean Style

Ingredients

1/2 teaspoon salt

1 lb lean ground beef

1 onion, finely chopped

2 -4 garlic cloves, minced

1 (14 1/2 ounce) cans tomatoes

1 1/2 cups beef broth

1 teaspoon minced fresh oregano or 1/2 teaspoon crumbled dried oregano

1/4 teaspoon pepper

8 ounces dried orzo pasta (1 cup)

1 (10 ounce) packages frozen chopped spinach, thawed

1/2-3/4 cup grated parmesan cheese

Directions

Take a frying pan and sprinkle salt into it over moderately high temperature.

Take beef and crumble it into pan and cook, mix frequently, for three to five min. lower the temperature, mix in onion and keep on cooking, mix, for approximately five min. get rid of extra fat.

Take garlic, tomatoes and add them along with their liquid, pepper, oregano and broth.

Heat the mixture to boiling. Then mix in pasta.

Lower the temperature, cover it and let it simmer for approximately ten to twelve min, or till pasta gets soften.

Then take spinach and squeeze out liquid as much as possible. Then mix spinach and pasta mixture or till heated through.

You can serve this recipe with cheese to add according to your taste and choice.

Mediterranean Chicken Breasts with Avocado Tapenade

Ingredients

4 boneless skinless chicken breast halves

1 tablespoon grated lemon peel

5 tablespoons fresh lemon juice, divided

2 tablespoons olive oil, divided

1 teaspoon olive oil, divided

1 garlic clove, finely chopped

1/2 teaspoon salt

1/4 teaspoon ground black pepper

2 garlic cloves, roasted and mashed

1/2 teaspoon sea salt

1/4 teaspoon fresh ground pepper

1 medium tomato, seeded and finely chopped

1/4 cup small green pimento stuffed olive, thinly sliced

3 tablespoons capers, rinsed

2 tablespoons fresh basil leaves, finely sliced

1 large Hass avocado, ripe, finely chopped

Directions

Take a sealable plastic bag and combine in this bag, chicken and marinade of lemon peel, two tablespoons lemon juice, two tablespoons olive oil, garlic, salt and pepper.

Then seal the bag and keep in refrigerator for thirty min.

Then take a bowl, and whisk together rest of 3 tablespoons lemon juice, roasted garlic, remaining half teaspoons olive oil, sea salt and fresh ground pepper.

Then blend in tomato.

Then blend in green olives.

Then blend in capers.

Then blend in basil.

Then blend in avocado.

Keep aside.

Take the chicken out of bag and get rid of the marinade.

Then grill over moderately hot coals for four to five min on each side.

You can serve this recipe with Avocado Tapenade.

Mediterranean Appetizer Meals

Mediterranean Morsels

Ingredients

12 pimento stuffed olives, drained

5 ounces cherry tomatoes, preferably sweet grape variety, rinsed and patted dry

1 (14 ounce) cans cut hearts of palm, drained

4 ounces whole mushrooms, quartered

1/2 cup canned garbanzo beans, rinsed and drained

1 1/2 tablespoons extra virgin olive oil

1 tablespoon dried basil leaves

20 plain crisp breadsticks (4 x 1/2 inches)

Directions

Take all of the ingredients and mix them together besides breadsticks in gallon-sized plastic storage bag.

Then seal it firmly and shake well.

Then keep in refrigerator for approximately four hrs.

You can serve this recipe with breadsticks and wooden toothpicks.

Mediterranean Bruschetta

Ingredients

Really good quality country bread, like a sourdough

Extra virgin olive oil

Sea salt or kosher salt

Dried Mediterranean oregano

Directions

Take bread and slice it one inch thick.

Then after this, grill in the oven under grill till color changes to golden, it takes approximately one min on each side.

Use olive oil for drizzle.

Use sea salt, oregano as sprinkles.

Delicious.

Mediterranean Deviled Eggs

Ingredients

6 hard-cooked eggs, shelled

1/3 cup mayonnaise

1 tablespoon finely chopped onion

1 tablespoon capers, rinsed, drained, and chopped

2 teaspoons chopped pitted Kalamata olives

2 teaspoons Dijon mustard

1/4 teaspoon hot pepper sauce

Directions

First, take eggs and halve them lengthwise/longwise.

Then right after this, remove the yolks; press through a sieve in small size bowl.

Then blend in mayonnaise.

Then blend in onion.

Then blend in capers.

Then blend in olives.

Then blend in mustard.

Then blend in hot pepper sauce.

After this, take mixture and spoon it into egg white halves.

Then place it on plate, use plastic wrap for loosely covering, keep in refrigerator for a couple of hrs for chilling completely.

Decadent Mediterranean Honeyed Olive Oil Toasts

Ingredients

1 baguette, cut into 4 pieces

4 tablespoons olive oil

4 teaspoons honey (approx.)

1 pinch cardamom (one teeny shake)

1/16 teaspoon ground cumin

1/8 teaspoon dried mint flakes

1/2 teaspoon marjoram

Directions

Take dry spices and blend them together in small size dish.

Then take bread and chop into four pieces.

Take olive oil and brush it onto bread pieces.

Take honey and squash it onto every bread pieces horizontally in a line. Then spread it with the barbecue brush.

Then take the honey and blend it into breads.

Then after this, pinch the spice mix and spread onto the bread pieces.

Then take breads and put them on cookie sheet and toast for three to four min or till color is golden brown over the top.

Mediterranean Split Pea Dip

Ingredients

1 1/4 cups yellow split peas

1 small onion, coarsely chopped

1 small onion, very finely chopped

1 garlic clove, coarsely chopped

6 tablespoons extra virgin olive oil

1 tablespoon chopped fresh oregano

Salt & pepper

Chopped oregano (to garnish)

Savory biscuit, for serving

Directions

First, take the split peas and rinse them under running water.

Then place them in medium size pan.

Take the roughly chopped onion, garlic, plenty cold water and add them to the medium size pan.

Heat it to boiling, lower the temperature and let it simmer for approximately forty five min or till soften.

Drain well and put in either blender or food processor, serve some of the cooking liquid.

Take five tablespoons of oil and add it and process till smooth enough.

Take oregano and add it, adjust seasonings according to your taste and choice.

Shift the mixture to bowl.

Use finely chopped onion along with extra oregano as sprinkle.

Use the rest of oil as drizzle.

Serve deliciously.

Mediterranean Summer Breeze Shrimp Appetizer

Ingredients

3/4 lb large shrimp, shell and tail removed, deveined, cut lengthwise slightly (12 pieces)

1/2 teaspoon salt (or less optional)

2 teaspoons vinegar

6 garlic cloves, chopped finely

1/2 cup chopped tomato, chopped finely

3 tablespoons olive oil

1 teaspoon black pepper (peppercorns ground fine)

1/4 teaspoon cayenne pepper (or less optional)

1 teaspoon ground cumin

1 teaspoon dried tarragon

2 tablespoons dried oregano

4 tablespoons Kalamata olives, pits removed and coarsely chopped

2 tablespoons capers

4 tablespoons feta cheese, crumbled

4 tablespoons lemon juice

1 teaspoon ouzo (optional)

2 lemons, cut up into wedges

Directions

Take cleaned shrimp and place it in mixing bowl, take half teaspoon salt, vinegar and add them and toss well.

Prepare spice mixture from, half teaspoon salt, Black pepper, one tablespoon oregano, tarragon, ground cumin, cayenne pepper, keep aside.

Take separate plates and place on them, some chopped up olives, capers, crumbled feta cheese and lemon wedges on the side.

Take three tablespoons of olive oil and place it in pan, once hot, add chopped tomatoes along with garlic to the pan.

Mix for thirty seconds.

Take shrimp and add it to pan.

Use a part of spice mixture as sprinkle over the top of every shrimp.

Once shrimps changes color to pink, one time turn them over and fry the other side.

Take the balance of spices mixture and add to the top of shrimp.

Take some of the garlic/tomato and put some of it from the top on top.

Once the 2nd side turns pink in color, use generous quantity of dry oregano as sprinkle over every shrimp.

Then take shrimp and place it over the top of chopped olives along with feta cheese, capers, in separate plates.

Take some lemon juice and add it to every shrimp. Don't forget to add a very small quantity of ouzo.

Mediterranean Chicken Cracker Topper

Ingredients

1 cup cooked chicken breast, chopped (boneless, skinless, 5 oz.)

1 medium red pepper

1/2 cup light mayonnaise

2 green onions, sliced

1/4 cup hydrated sun-dried tomato, chopped

1/2 teaspoon Italian seasoning

Cracker

Directions

Take all of the above mentioned ingredients and blend them together till well mixed.

Then cover it and keep in refrigerator for a minimum of sixty min.

Use one teaspoon chicken mixture for topping every cracker.

You can serve this recipe right away.

Mediterranean Mayonnaise

Ingredients

3 egg yolks

1 tablespoon lemon juice

1/2 teaspoon Dijon mustard

1 teaspoon coarse salt

1/2 cup canola oil

1 1/4 cups canola oil

1/4 cup extra virgin olive oil

2 tablespoons hot water

2 teaspoons lemon juice

1 teaspoon salt

Finely chopped rosemary (or basil)

Directions

Take egg yolks and beat them on moderate speed till slightly thicken.

Take lemon juice and add it.

Then take mustard and add it.

Then take salt and add it.

Then beat for one min.

Raise the speed to moderately high.

Take half cup oil and add it (don't forget to add one teaspoon at a single time).

Take the rest of oils and pour them in, beat for ten min or mixed.

Then right after this, fold in water, lemon juice, and salt.

Right after this, fold in either rosemary or basil.

You cans serve this recipe at room temperature or keep in refrigerator for up to seven days.

Mediterranean Grilled Chicken Fingers

Ingredients

3 chicken breasts

2 shallots

1 tablespoon fresh parsley

1 lemon

1 (1 ounce) package Hidden Valley Original Ranch Seasoning Mix

1 tablespoon dried oregano

Salt or pepper

1/2 cucumber

12 ounces Greek yogurt

3 tablespoons grated parmesan cheese

1 teaspoon dried dill

1 teaspoon fresh chives

Olive oil flavored cooking spray

Directions

For Preparing Chicken Strips.

Take chicken breast and slice it thin and fine and then chop into strips.

Then shallots, parsley and chop them finely, squeeze the juice of lemon and blend well in large size bowl.

Take Hidden Valley Original Ranch Seasoning Mix, oregano, salt and pepper and add these ingredients to the mix and blend well

Take chicken strips and place them in a plastic food bag and don't forget to pour in the mixture.

After closing the bag, shake well.

Keep in refrigerator for sixty min or for a night.

For Preparing Dipping Sauce.

Take half of the cucumber, peel, and seed and puree it then after this, combine it in a medium size bowl with Greek yogurt along with chives, parmesan cheese, and dried dill.

Keep the mixture in refrigerator for a minimum of sixty min or for a night.

Preparations.

Take a large size grill pan and spray it with cooking spray and then heat it moderately.

Then take chicken strips and place them and grill for approximately three min on every side.

Once brown place them in tray for serving.

Take dipping sauce and place it in bowl and then place on serving tray with the chicken strips.

Alouette Crumbled Feta Mediterranean Caponata

Ingredients

1/4 cup virgin olive oil

1 cup onion, chopped in 1/2-inch dice

1 tablespoon pine nuts

1 medium eggplant, cut into 1/2-inch cubes (to yield 2 cups)

1/4 cup green olives, chopped

1/4 teaspoon fresh thyme leave

1/4 cup diced tomato

1 ounce balsamic vinegar

1 container feta, mediterranean cheese from alouette

Directions

Take large size frying pan, and heat olive oil in it over moderate temperature.

Then take pine nuts, onions and add them and fry for four to five min or till tender.

Then take eggplant and add it, keep on cooking for five extra min.

Then take thyme, chopped tomato and add them.

Then take olives, balsamic vinegar and add them

Heat the mixture to boiling.

Reduce the temperature and let the mixture simmer for approximately four to five min.

Take away from heat and let it cool.

Then right after this, fold in Alouette® Feta Mediterranean Crumbles.

Serve deliciously.

Alouette Mediterranean Bruschetta

Ingredients

1 loaf French bread, sliced

4 ounces extra virgin olive oil

2 teaspoons freshly chopped parsley

1 lb pre-cooked cocktail shrimp

1 (6 1/2 ounce) packages alouette sundried tomato & basil

Directions

First, heat the grill.

Take olive oil, and mix it with one teaspoon of chopped parsley and then brush on both sides of slices of French bread.

After this, grill them for one to two min on every side till crunchy and then allow to cool.

Take Alouette® Sundried Tomato & Basil and spread them equally over the French bread slices.

Use already cooked shrimp for topping.

Use the rest of chopped parsley as sprinkle.

Roasted Red Pepper
& Feta Dip

Ingredients

4 red bell peppers

1/4 cup extra virgin olive oil

3 garlic cloves, peeled

2 cups crumbled feta cheese

1 teaspoon smoked paprika

1/2 teaspoon chili pepper flakes

1 tablespoon lemon juice

1/4 cup parsley

Olive (to garnish)

Directions

First, char peppers in the broiler till gets black on every side.

Then close in paper bag for approximately ten min.

Then take peppers, peel and seed them.

After this, take all of the ingredients and puree them in the processor along with peppers.

Use salt, peppers for seasonings.

Let it chill for a minimum of three hrs or for a night.

Mediterranean White Bean Spread with Fresh Herbs

Ingredients

1 (15 ounce) cans white kidney beans, rinsed and drained (cannellini)

3 cloves garlic

1 1/2 tablespoons lime juice

1 tablespoon olive oil

1 tablespoon basil, fresh, snipped into medium size pieces

1 tablespoon thyme, fresh

1/4 teaspoon salt, to taste

1/4 teaspoon fresh ground black pepper, to taste

Directions

Take a food processor or blender and put beans, olive oil, lime, garlic in this processor for processing till smooth enough.

Take the rest of ingredients and add them. Blend well.

Keep in refrigerator for a couple of hrs or for a night.

Seven Layer Mediterranean Dip
with
Rosemary Butter Flatbread

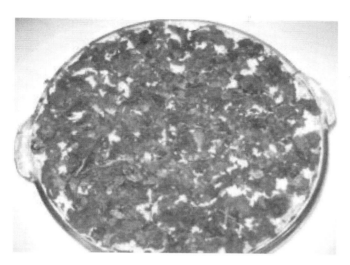

Ingredients

Wild Mushroom Couscous

1 cup plain cooked couscous

2 tablespoons lemon juice

2 tablespoons olive oil

4 -5 shiitake mushrooms, soaked and chopped

2 medium tomatoes, seeded and chopped

1/3 cup green onion, diced

1/4 cup pine nuts

1 tablespoon oregano

Spicy Lemon Hummus

8 ounces prepared lemon hummus

1 tablespoon ground cumin

Fresh ground black pepper

Kalamata Olive Tapenade

3 garlic cloves

1 cup pitted Kalamata olive

1 cup pine nuts

1 cup parsley, minced

1/2 cup cilantro, minced

1 teaspoon fresh rosemary

Fresh ground black pepper

1 teaspoon orange peel, grated

1/4 cup olive oil

2 (6 ounce) jars marinated artichoke hearts, drained and chopped

8 ounces feta cheese, crumbled

4 ounces sun-dried tomatoes, drained and chopped

1 cup parsley, minced

Flatbread with Rosemary Butter

5 loaves prepared flat bread

2 tablespoons butter, melted

2 teaspoons fresh rosemary

Directions

1st Prepare the Wild Mushroom Couscous.

Take one cup of plain couscous as instructed on the package. Then allow to cool.

Then take olive oil, lemon juice and whisk them together.

Then pour into couscous.

Take the next five ingredients and add them, blend well.

Use wild mushrooms couscous for lining glass pie plate.

2nd Prepare the Spicy Lemon Hummus.

Take ground cumin, black pepper and blend them in prepared lemon hummus.

Take the spicy lemon hummus and spread over the top of couscous mixture.

3rd Prepare the Kalamata Olive Tapenade.

Take garlic and mince it in food processor.

Then take the next seven ingredients and add them.

Then take olive oil and add it while blade is running. Process well till smooth enough.

Take one cup of tapenade and spread it over hummus layer.

Take chopped artichoke hearts and arrange them as the next layer, then layer the feta, then sundried tomatoes then parsley.

You can serve this recipe right away or keep in refrigerator.

4th Prepare the Flatbread with Rosemary Butter.

Take rosemary and mix it into melted butter and then brush it on flatbread.

Heat on baking tray for approximately two min at three hundred fifty (350) degrees Fahrenheit.

Feta Cheese Log
with
Kalamata Olives and Sun-Dried Tomatoes

Ingredients

8 ounces feta cheese, crumbled

4 ounces cream cheese, softened

2 tablespoons extra virgin olive oil

1 small garlic clove, minced

1/2 teaspoon dried Mediterranean oregano, crumbled

1/8-1/4 teaspoon cayenne pepper (depending on your taste)

1/4 cup chopped Kalamata olive

1/4 cup chopped sun-dried tomato

Garnish

1/2 cup chopped walnuts, toasted

1/4 cup minced fresh parsley

Directions

First, take feta, oil, cream cheese and blend them together in a mixer on moderate speed till well mixed.

Take the rest of ingredients and add them, blend well.

Then form log shape approximately ten inch long.

Then take parsley, walnuts and combine them, and roll cheese log in this mixture, for sticking the walnuts and parsley, press slightly to the sides of log.

Use plastic wrap for wrapping and keep in refrigerator for a minimum of five hrs prior to serving.

Get rid of plastic wrap and then lay it on serving platter that has been lined with parsley.

You can serve this recipe with assorted crackers and toasted baguette slices.

Mediterranean Salad Meals

Mediterranean Salad in Minutes

Ingredients

Dressing

1/4 cup vegetable oil

1/8 cup lemon juice

1 teaspoon brown sugar

1/2 teaspoon baby capers, drained and rinsed

1/2 teaspoon Dijon mustard

1/2 teaspoon unsweetened mayonnaise

Salad

10 -15 Kalamata olives, pitted and halved

10 -15 radishes, halved

1 small red onion, chopped

1/2 cup feta, crumbled (or more)

1 seedless cucumber, quartered lengthwise and sliced

1 medium green pepper, chopped (capsicum)

10 -15 cherry tomatoes, halved

Directions

First of all, take the items for dressing in this recipe and combine these together.

Then take the items for salad in this recipe and prepare them as noted above.

Then take the dressing and add it and toss well.

Delicious recipe is ready.

Farfalle (Bow Tie) Pasta Salad

Ingredients

6 cups farfalle pasta, uncooked

2/3 cup olive oil

1 (15 ounce) cans cannellini beans or 1 (15 ounce) cans navy beans, drained and rinsed

1 (15 ounce) cans red kidney beans, drained and rinsed

1 (7 ounce) containers roasted red peppers or 1 (7 ounce) containers pimientos, drained and sliced into strips

1/2 cup onion, finely chopped

1/2 cup fresh parsley, finely chopped

1/3 cup red wine vinegar

2 garlic cloves, minced

Salt and pepper, to taste

Directions

Take pasta and boil it for twelve min or till ready and done.

And then rinse it and then drain it

Allow to rest for five min.

Then mix in oil.

Take the cooled pasta along with seasoning and beans and add them; toss well so that the items are mixed.

Then keep in refrigerator, covered, for two hrs.

Mediterranean Tuna Salad

Ingredients

1 English cucumber, pre-wrapped

10 ounces drained and flaked light chunk tuna in water

1/3 cup pitted Kalamata olive, chopped

2 small tomatoes, chopped

3 tablespoons of bottled olive oil vinaigrette (salad dressing)

Lettuce greens or toasted French baguette

Directions

Take cucumber and chop it into chunks.

Take the Kalamata olives, olive oil, chopped tomatoes, tuna, and chopped cucumber and combine these items with vinaigrette salad dressing. Blend well.

You can serve this recipe over lettuce greens.

You can also deliciously serve this recipe on toasted baguettes.

White Bean and Tuna Salad

Ingredients

1 (16 ounce) cans cannellini beans, drained and rinsed

3 (6 ounce) cans tuna, packed in water, drained

1 red onion, chopped finely

3 tablespoons lemon juice

2 tablespoons red wine vinegar

2 tablespoons balsamic vinegar

4 tablespoons olive oil

4 garlic cloves, minced

2 tablespoons fresh herbs, chopped

Salt and pepper

Directions

Take the liquid items for this recipe, pepper, salt, garlic and whisk them together.

Take the rest of items for this recipe and add them and mix them together.

Keep in refrigerator for a minimum of two hrs.

Mediterranean Fruit Salad

Ingredients

12 seedless grapes

1 pear

1 apple

1 peach

2 kiwi fruits

1 orange

Plain fat-free yogurt

Directions

Take the fruits items above and chop them first and then 2nd take these chopped fruits items and blend them together with yogurt and allow to chill.

Delicious salad is ready.

Barbecue Lamb on Mediterranean Salad

Ingredients

400 g lamb fillets or 400 g boneless lamb loin

1 tablespoon olive oil

1/2 lemon, juice of

1 tablespoon balsamic vinegar

1 tablespoon chopped oregano or 1 tablespoon thyme

1 garlic clove, finely chopped

60 g feta cheese, crumbled

1 red capsicum

100 g mixed lettuce leaves

12 Kalamata olives

Directions

Take lemon juice, balsamic vinegar, oil and whisk these items together and take the half of mixture and put it to one side.

Take oregano, garlic and add them to the rest of mixture.

Then take the mixture and pour it over lamb pieces.

Then marinate lamb for twenty min.

Take the capsicum and grill it till skin becomes black in color as well as blisters.

Then take it out and put in plastic bag for five min.

For not letting steam to escape, seal the top of bag.

Then after this, take the capsicum out from bag and hold it under water so the black skin is removed.

Then take this cleaned capsicum and chop it into strips and keep aside.

Then grill the lamb for five min on every side, use marinade for basting.

Then allow the lamb to sit for five min.

Take lettuce, capsicum, feta, olive and assemble these items as 'stack' on every dish.

Take the pieces of lamb and add them to the lamb's top.

Then pour the rest of oil as well as vinegar mixture.

My Style Mediterranean Couscous Salad

Ingredients

3/4 cup chicken broth

1 cup couscous, uncooked

2 tablespoons olive oil

15 ounces artichoke hearts, chopped coarsely

10 ounces canned diced tomatoes

3 green chilies, chopped

1/2 cup feta cheese, crumbled

1/4 cup pine nuts, toasted

1/4 cup olive (Kalamata nice)

2 green onions, chopped

1 teaspoon garlic, chopped

2 tablespoons basil, fresh chopped

2 tablespoons mint, fresh chopped

2 tablespoons parsley, fresh chopped

Romaine lettuce or baby spinach leaves

Directions

Take broth and heat it to boiling and blend in couscous.

Then cover it properly and bring it back to boiling and then take it away from temperature and allow to sit for five min.

Use olive to drizzle and fluff by using fork and let cool.

Take all of the items besides romaine or baby spinach and combine them together and toss them.

You can serve this recipe over lettuce.

You can also serve this delicious recipe over spinach.

Mediterranean Cracked Wheat Salad

Ingredients

2 cups cracked wheat

1 1/2 cups chicken stock, heated

1/4 cup olive oil

3 tablespoons lemon juice or 3 tablespoons lime juice

2 bunches scallions, sliced

1 garlic clove, minced

1 cup feta cheese, crumbled

1 English cucumber, diced

1 (6 ounce) cans pitted ripe olives, sliced

1/4 cup fresh mint, chopped

1/3 cup cilantro, chopped

2 bell peppers, roasted &sliced

Salt and pepper

Directions

Take the cracked wheat and rinse it and place it in a bowl.

Take hot broth and add it and cover it and allow to rest for twenty to twenty five min or all of the liquid is assimilated and absorbed.

Allow to cool and fluff, from time to time, with the fork.

Take scallions, mint and add them.

Take cilantro, cucumber and add them.

Take the olives, roasted pepper and add them.

Blend them well.

Take olive oil, salt, pepper, lemon juice, garlic and blend them together and add it to the salad.

Then blend in feta cheese.

Then keep in refrigerator, covered, till serving time.

Mediterranean Antipasti

Ingredients

4 green asparagus spears or 4 white asparagus, cooked

1 hardboiled egg

1 artichoke heart

1 plum tomato

2 slices prosciutto ham, rolled

2 ounces pickled red cabbage

2 ounces albacore tuna, drained

2 ounces provolone cheese or 2 ounces Monterey jack cheese, cut into 2 slices

2 -3 leaves iceberg lettuce or 2 -3 leaves red leaf lettuce or 2 -3 leaves green leaf lettuce

Basil vinaigrette or any other vinaigrette dressing

Directions

Use lettuce leaves for lining the plate.

Take hardboiled egg and chop it in half.

Take the other ingredients for this recipe and arrange them on plate. Also include egg.

You can serve this delicious recipe with vinaigrette dressing.

Two Bean & Artichoke Salad

Ingredients

1 (15 ounce) cans garbanzo beans, drained & rinsed

3 tablespoons extra virgin olive oil

2 -3 tablespoons balsamic vinegar

1/4 cup chopped fresh parsley

2 teaspoons dried Mediterranean oregano

1/2 teaspoon black pepper

1/2 teaspoon salt

1 (15 ounce) cans red kidney beans, drained & rinsed

1 (14 ounce) cans artichoke hearts, drained & coarsely chopped

4 green onions, trimmed & chopped

2 large tomatoes, diced

1 cup frozen corn kernels, thawed under hot running water

4 garlic cloves, minced

Directions

Take all of the above items for this recipe and combine them together in large size bowl and keep in refrigerator half to one hour.

You can serve this tasty and delicious recipe over shredded lettuce bread along with pita.

You can also serve this recipe with pita chips.

Orzo Salad with Corn

Ingredients

1 lb orzo pasta

2 cups fresh corn kernels, cut off the cob

1 cup finely chopped red sweet bell pepper

1 cup Kalamata olive, pitted, cut in half

1/4 cup thinly sliced scallion

2 tablespoons coarsely chopped basil

2 tablespoons drained capers

1/4 cup packed fresh parsley leaves, finely chopped

1/4 cup olive oil

3 tablespoons wine vinegar

1/8 teaspoon salt

Fresh ground black pepper, to taste

Fresh edible flower, such as fresh nasturtium

Directions

Take light salted water in large size pot and heat it to boiling.

Take orzo and add it and cook for seven min, mixing from time to time, or till soften.

Then drain it well and shift it to large size bowl.

Take scallions, olives, pepper, corn and add these items. And toss them well.

Take salt, pepper, vinegar, oil, parsley, capers, basil and add them and toss lightly.

Delicious recipe can decorated with the edible flowers.

Tahini Dressing over Mediterranean Salad

Ingredients

Dressing

4 tablespoons sesame tahini

2 small garlic cloves, minced

1 tablespoon fresh parsley, finely chopped

1 tablespoon fresh chives, finely chopped

1/2 teaspoon brown sugar (optional)

4 tablespoons extra virgin olive oil

2 tablespoons lemon juice, freshly squeezed

1/8 cup capers, minced

1/8 cup Kalamata olive, minced

Paprika (to garnish)

Salt and pepper, to taste

Salad

1 medium tomato, sliced

1 bell pepper, sliced (any color)

1 cup chickpeas, cooked and cooled (or canned)

1/2 medium red onion, sliced

1/4 cup feta cheese, crumbled

Directions

Take the items for dressing and blend them together in bowl.

You can also add brown sugar if you like to be little bit sweet.

Take the veggies and slice them for salad.

Take chickpeas and add them and place in the plate.

Add salt as well as pepper according to your own choice and preference.

Use feta cheese as sprinkle.

Take the dressing and add it.

You serve the delicious and tasty dressing over grains and falafels.

Wild Rice & Pasta with Sun-Dried Tomatoes

Ingredients

0.5 (1 lb.) box gemelli pasta, cooked al dente

1 (14 ounce) cans cooked wild rice, drained

1/2 red bell pepper, diced small

1/2 green bell pepper, diced small

1/2 cup sun-dried tomato, chopped

1/2 cup Kalamata olive, sliced

6 -8 scallions, with some greens, chopped

1/2 cup pine nuts, toasted

3 -4 large garlic cloves, minced

Salt & pepper

1/2 cup extra virgin olive oil (approx.)

3 tablespoons balsamic vinegar (approx.)

1/4 cup fresh basil, chopped

Directions

Take the 1st NINE items for this recipe and combine them together in large size bowl.

Take olive oil, vinegar to drizzle over the mixture. Mix well.

Continue to add vinegar as well as oil till each item of the recipe is moisten.

Take salt, pepper and add them according to your own taste and choice.

Use basil as sprinkle.

Keep in refrigerator for a few hrs.

Then pull out and mix.

Delicious.

Mediterranean Chickpea Salad

Ingredients

28 ounces chickpeas, rinsed and drained

7 ounces roasted red peppers, drained and chopped

1/2 small red onion, minced

1/4 cup fresh parsley, chopped

2 1/2 tablespoons lemon juice, bottled is fine

2 tablespoons extra virgin olive oil

2 teaspoons Dijon mustard

2 garlic cloves, minced, jarred is fine

Salt

Pepper

Directions

Take all of the items for this recipe and blend them together in a bowl.

Keep in refrigerator for a minimum of half hour. I recommend to keep it in the refrigerator for longer time.

Mediterranean Spinach Salad

Ingredients

1 package feta cheese

1 bag spinach

2 tablespoons Kalamata olive juice

1 tablespoon olive oil

1 tablespoon balsamic vinegar

Directions

Take spinach, six teaspoons of Kalamata olive juice and put them together in Ziploc bag and shake the bag.

Then take the rest of juice out from bag and put the spinach in the bowl.

Take balsamic vinegar, olive oil and blend them together and then toss this mixture into spinach.

Take feta and chop it thin and fine and then place in along with salad.

Blend together and deliciously serve this recipe.

If you enjoy the recipes in this little recipe book, please take the time to share your thoughts and post a review on Amazon. It'd be greatly appreciated!

Thank you and good luck!

Victoria Love

www.AfflatusPublishing.com

www.epicdetox.com

www.secretstoweightlossrevealed.com

Check Out Some of My Other Books

Below you'll find some of my other popular books that are popular on Amazon and Kindle as well. You can visit my author page on Amazon to see other work done by me.

Paleo: The Caveman's Paleo For Beginners: Amazing! The Ultimate Paleo Diet for Beginner's Blueprint for Incredible Caveman's Revenge Paleo Cookbook: 41 Red Hot Melt The Pounds Fast Weight Loss Recipes Uncovered With Your Top Paleo Diet Questions Answered In Never Before Seen Detail

10 Day Green Smoothie Cleansing: The Ultimate Lose 10 Pounds in 10 Days Green Smoothie Detox Blueprint

10 Day Detox Diet: Innovative Diet Plan Transforms Your Life, Instantly Giving You Explosive Energy and Vitality Guaranteed

Vegetarian Slow Cooker Recipes Revealed: Fast Recipes For Slow Delicious Success

Cooking Light in 3 Steps; Cooking Light Has Never Been So Easy; Super-Fast and Light Done Right Cooking Revealed, Simple 3 Step Recipes, Fast Cooking Done Right

Famous Recipes Cookbook; Rediscover 70 All-Time Super Star Classic Recipes

If the links do not work, for whatever reason, you can simply search for these titles on the Amazon website to find them.

Bonus: FREE Ebooks!

As a preferred client of Afflatus Publishing we strive to provide more value, all the time. As you are now a special part of our family we want to let you in on a little a little secret...

A special thanks goes out to you. So subscribe to our free e-book giveaway. Each week we will spotlight an amazing new title. **Yours absolutely free**.

Click Here to Subscribe For Free Now.

If that link doesn't work click here:

https://afflatus.leadpages.net/free-ebook/

Printed in Great Britain
by Amazon.co.uk, Ltd.,
Marston Gate.